Myrrh/My Life As A Screamer

Judith Roche

For Robert –

for the river – the one poem
we are all writing our own part
to –
Judith R.

9-94

The following poems were previously published in these magazines: "Thunder After Thunder" in *A Gathering of Poets* (anthology); "Helen: When They Called Her Witch" and "Dendrites," *Rhowedder;* "Alternate Insomnia at the Lake in Winter," *Willow Springs;* "The Night We Hollered Down the Dell," *Duckabush Journal;* "The Release," *The American Voice;* "Desire in Laughing Seascape," and "Her Story," *Ellensburg Anthology;* "Desire," *Yellow Silk;* "Anatomy and Destiny," *Bumbershoot Anthology;* "April," *Red Lines,* "The Sound I Learned from my Mother's Song," *Clay Drum;* "Green River," *15 Seattle Book;* "Letter Home When Home Has Shifted on Her Haunches," and "Dancing Dreams My Mother Had," *Open Sky;* "Trying the Ways We Know," *Backbone.*

Cover art by Deborah Mersky

Published by Black Heron Press
P.O. Box 95676
Seattle, Washington 98145

Dedication

HOT BONES

This is for my son, Robin,
whose chromosomes count too many
and whose ears are stopped
by the word *profound*,
who speaks with his hands,
even in the delirium of a high fever,
and who has images of *hot bones*
in his poems, which he performs
in the flourish of a fervid dance,
accompanied by a tambourine he doesn't hear,
the swirling from inside
his own strong internal rhythm,
his eyes seeing a poetry of agile hands
connected to body, to honest work
    — stacking wood or sorting scrap metal —
which is his passion,
tied, as it is, to trust
in the rightness of giving oneself
wholly, to the task at hand.

CONTENTS

"*Myrrh*: Murmur of Life," by Sharon Doubiago   3

HOT BONES

Myrrh   13

Trying the Ways We Know   14

Desire   15

Why She Went to the Woods   16

We Balance Each Other's Night and Daylight Needs   17

They Think About Escape   19

Aerial Escape   20

Anatomy and Destiny   21

Letter Home When Home Has Shifted on Her Haunches   22

Basement   24

Camille   25

She Searches   27

The Sound I Learned from My Mother's Song   28

Alternate Insomnia at the Lake in Winter   29

Night Passage   30

Desire in Laughing Seascape   32

Helen: When They Called Her Witch   34

Dendrites   36

Love in a Lifeboat   38

Helen: The Questions   39

But It Takes Till Then   41

Dancing Dreams My Mother Had, I in Utero   42

Myrrha   43

BETWEEN PATTERN AND RANDOM SCATTER

Three   46

After Sleep   47

Circles   48

Requiem   50

The Release   52

Green River   54

After the Revolution   56

The Open Book Comes Off the Page   58

Thunder After Thunder, Returning Like Rhyme   60

Social Security   61

TRYING THE WAYS WE KNOW

Trying the Ways We Know, Part II   65

April   66

The Flowers   67

The Night We Hollered Down the Tunnel in the Dell   68

The Forest at Night and on Into   69

The Bones of the Priestess Loom Large on the Beach   70

The Bait   71

Lovers   73

The White Horse Girl and the Blue Wind Boy   75

Petroglyph Poem   77

Changing on the Road   81

Letter to Li T'ai-Po   83

Pinnipedia   84

My Life in Letters   85

We Take a Night Boat Ride Together   86

Parthenos   87

Mnemosyne   89

MY LIFE AS A SCREAMER

My Life as a Screamer   91

Hostia   99

MYRRH: MURMUR OF LIFE

The Eternal Persons of the Poem: Judith Roche

Thunder after thunder, returning like rhyme, she is coming across the lawn at Fort Worden with, finally, the first biography of H.D. (*H.D., The Life and Work of an American Poet,* by Janice S. Robinson). "The reddest rose unfolds . . . ." H.D. was the first poet I read, at 19. From the inspiration I proceeded to get an education, but never, through graduate school, did a professor so much as mention H.D. We read (and read about) her lovers, husband, boyfriends, therapists, editors, publishers, etc. (Pound, Aldington, Lawrence, Williams, Ford, Ellis, Freud, Robeson, Laughlin, etc.). Now Judith — Hermes, Messenger of the Gods — brings me the missing pieces, carries forth the story that opened my poet destiny so many years before. We sit under an enormous red cedar, we are always under that tree. We bond, each the One the other has waited for: a female, literary soul mate.

In the fall of 1983 Judith Roche moved from Seattle to San Francisco for two years to study at New College with Diane di Prima and Robert Duncan. As she put it in her first letter to me: "R.D. dominates all thought and talk here . . . but is himself overshadowed by the memory of Charles Olson who is shadowed in a larger circle by Pound . . . Another shadow slightly off-center but very present is H.D."

Coincidentally, Duncan happens to be the first poet I ever saw read, in 1965 — he read his Psyche poem ("A Poem Beginning with a Line by Pindar") — his connection to H.D. unknown to me. And, yes, Olson, whose poetics I studied for ten years before making my escape, necessary to becoming a poet myself, being female and so marginalized even the Poet of Margins wouldn't have recognized me. "God does not weave a loose web, no," H.D. says.

So the bond between Judith and me deepened: through the 80s, now the 90s, she and I over her kitchen table, high in the trees over Lake Washington ("I am Helen of the Trees, / which means they hang me from them"), countless, passionate nights "hammering out our poetics," and our poems, stories, essays, and classes, as if the Muse really is a woman.

3

(Judith's thesis from New College is the published "Myrrh: A Study of Persona in H.D.'s *Trilogy*"; *Line*, 12: Fall 1988.)

Sound, Soul, Personae

The experience at New College was a profound study of the Truth all poets begin with but most lose in mainstream schooling: the fact of *gnosis within language*. "It is not in our own powers but in the powers of the words we are to work," Duncan tirelessly explained. "To occupy the *office of poetry* is to live under the *orders of the poem*." This is radically different from the aesthetic of most contemporary poetry, though not from mainstream West Coast ecofeminist consciousness. "Humanity did not weave the web of life," Chief Seattle says. "We are merely a strand of it. Whatever we do to the web, we do to ourselves."

Roche follows the orders of the poem rather than making the poem bend to her will. When one realizes how profoundly *Myrrh* comes from this practice on all levels (a few of which I want to point out here), how successfully she pulls off one of the riskiest of endeavors — risky because we have so few examples of this from the contemporary psyche (at best we have poets in a holding pattern, though more often poets in blind reaction) — one begins to grasp a true greatness, a highly original, courageous, mature, beautiful singularity of Voice, Theme, Sound, Image, etc., making up a brilliant whole. *Integrity* is from the Latin root *integer*: wholeness.

Primary in the "orders of the poem" is sound. "The deepest ground the ground of sound" is again a profoundly different (and therefore possibly disturbing) aesthetic from that of the little short stories with psycho-philosophical messages so commonly accepted everywhere now as poetry. Some people are visuals, some kinesthetics, some are audio-tonals, and some are digitals, so I'm not sure that sound *is* the deepest ground for those who are not audio-tonals, but the question here is, *is sound the ground of all true poetry?* Outside the Duncan/Olson/Pound/H.D. tradition, and the little lip service given to "musicality," sound has remained an almost unconscious phenomenon in our discipline, hardly a subject of study — perhaps we're "recognizing" it when we "hear" "innate talent." Personally I believe that poets do start with the ground of sound, as in how we learn language as infants, by sound and rhythm, not by reading or sight. Then we get waylaid in schooling, losing the germ of sound, shamed into producing visual/digital poems that lend themselves to the grading system. (Why *has* the century been such a visual one? Electricity? The image has certainly dictated 20th century poetry — the first revolution: banishment of rhyme. Sound, at least any indulgence/celebration of it, is almost taboo, certainly one's own sounds are, which in their deep interior source and/or subjectivity are more difficult to control (critique) than the printed word.)

Myrrh is as much *about* sound as it *is* sound. Roche enters language organically, enters organic language without shame (though shame is a theme here and may be, to an extent, a by-product of her daring), and so for us to enter these poems is to experience *growing sound*. She submerges deep into the Body of language and sound until the intense interior opens out into the vast sea beneath All — how often the Couple goes out in a boat in *Myrrh* — into the story of all Time, Being. Into the Music of the Spheres.

"She searches for the secret signs in the language," — Roche is writing here of H.D., but this is also a description of her own practice — "in the rhythmic associative babble of sound and murmur, *and the secret soul hidden in the words,* and how they go together, the 'little boxes conditioned to hatch butterflies.'" The notion (gnosis) that words have souls is not mainstream thought, either. "No word for gull has wings," an acclaimed poet says from that aesthetic. "But poets believe," I tell children, "that the meaning of your name is in the sound itself. Whether you are conscious or not of its meaning, your soul hears it, knows it, leads you to live out the story heard in the sound."

"All deep things are Song. See deep enough and you see musically" (Duncan). Over and over in *Myrrh* we experience this synesthesia, mainly of sight and sound. "Unsound the shadow/of a sob," "silhouetting our loud sound," "It's me in love with the sweet sax love line/they forget/silence between the notes,/ *Phanos* . . ." Sound is shaped by form — "the ear hears in its chambered whorl" — which we know by sight and feel. *Myrrh* is dedicated to Judith's deaf son, Robin, who is "accompa-

5

nied by a tambourine he doesn't hear,/the swirling from inside/his own strong internal rhythm." Sing deep enough and all the senses sing.

Primary in *Myrrh* also, and one with its *gnosis in language* aesthetic, is the idea of the Eternal Persons of the Poem. "The gods are real," said Pound, "they're states of mind." "We, as living poets," says Judith by way of Duncan by way of the Australian Aborigine belief/practice in the Eternal Persons of the Dream, "are weaving the stories of the Eternal Persons. We act out these stories in our lives. The poem tells these stories."

"The Personae . . . become possible when we move from a Newtonian to an Einsteinean world and the perception of time and causality shifts. The self is no longer separable from phenomenon because the act of observing changes the thing observed" ("Myrrh: A Study of Persona . . ." p. 103).

Myrrh is crowded with Eternal Persons, Gods and Goddesses, forces and archetypes. The greatest poems may be the hypnogogic ones, the state by which they come easiest.

mornings they crowd in
. . .
they erase my antecedent and place
my position somewhere else
a point beyond in air
referent to what I don't know

There are so many dream poems that Dream (Old English: joy, music) itself is an Eternal Person, bringing the news from the world beyond language, institution, waking thought.

But it is Myrrha herself who is most brilliantly evoked and brought to us in a new and important incarnation.

6

The Myrrh: Love, Desire, Sex, Death, the Unsatiable

"A girl in bad trouble," cursed by a minor goddess to be consumed with "unnatural lust" for her father, tricks him into sleeping with her while her mother is away at the Festival of Demeter. After nine nights he finally recognizes his daughter. He grabs his sword to kill her but in her flight she "turns into a tree/breaks open to birth" Adonis, who "becomes beloved of love" herself (Aphrodite). Myrrha not only produces the God of Love but the bitter tears of this experience, too. The myrrh. "Myrrh is still measured in 'tears'" ("Myrrh: A Study of Persona . . . ," p. 89).

The Myrrh (Mary) is clearly a seed myth for the "incestuous" Mary/God-Her-Father/Jesus myth, even down to the mysterious tree: Adonis' birth from the side of Myrrha the tree is mirrored in Jesus' death on the Myrtle tree (a return to the mother). ("Myrrh looks two ways at once,/can go in any direction.") The Myrrh is a change-over myth from matriarchal consciousness of early Mediterranean history to the patriarchal — Ovid making Freud's classic reversal, father/daughter-son rape being the True Story of the Patriarchy. In H.D.'s *Flowering of the Rod* , the "other" Mary, the sinner-prostitute Mary Magdalene "appears" to Kaspar, the Magi, *because* he is carrying myrrh to the New Child. This holy substance is the miraculous "lifeforce," the *elan vital,* the Love that saves the world. Myrrha "shall be . . . a name for an everlasting sign that shall not be cut off" (Isaiah, 55: 13). "She becomes Mary the Virgin [and all the other Marys in this story, i.e., the soul in the name] who *bears the bundle of myrrh* which carries the trace of the Son, of Jesus and Adonis, but is not the Son. Like Hermes, the Messenger, bringer of art and healing [and like the Virgin who births a child], this Child embodies both male and female. The Myrrh, as Eternal Person, brings both genders together, both archaic mother language and secondary paternal language, body and spirit, sensuality and healing, and Love, to an awaiting world" ("Myrrh: A Study of Persona . . . ," p. 109).

Myrrha is the Everlasting One who delivers us through the time of the Patriarchy. "Traditionally, there is no love poetry in Western Literature from 600 B.C. until the late 12th century, an omission of 1800 years," Judith says. The decree against love poetry is sustained strenuously in the teaching proclamations of our most acclaimed 20th century poets, e.g., Rilke, Roethke, Pound, Snyder, and taught *ad nauseum* by unloving teachers to young poets just moved by love to write their first poems. Love itself is forbidden.

"Whatever it is we are trying to get to in the poem, it's about love," Judith says. "Our primal experience is of trying to learn, to feel, to know, to enter this incredible universe—to make love to it, to join it. Language is the poet's way to it. The poem is an attempt to go through language— we can only get closer to it, because of the imprecision of language. We name things — these are states of grace, of beauty, of being — one state is Aphrodite, another is Aries. [But] by the very act of naming we know we are failing it."

Has anybody written so convincingly, so deeply, so meaningfully, so true and beautifully, of desire, as Judith Roche does in *Myrrh*?

I flamed about above my body
hovering as we do,
on the lip of the oscillation,
falling headlong into a language
we make up but there
before we are, clothing
ourselves in stories of "love"
for "grief," the various fictions
of unknown names swelling
urgent under the tongue. ("Night Passage")

But desire in *Myrrh* becomes the theme of the insatiable, an "unnatural lust," as Ovid puts it. "Let me perch on top,/a bird hovering, Isis-like, her search, for now, near sated." She searches, her desire is unsated because "desire itself/impulse enough." Can desire (which "has its [roots] in constellations of stars") be too much, be excessive when understood as the lifeforce? "Love tips the scale/towards life," even Stevens knew. Only our insatiable hunger keeps us here. It is much easier to die. The reason the daughter "can't get close enough" to the father is that EVERYTHING IN THE PATRIARCHY — Ovid to Jesus to Freud — HAS BEEN REVERSED. "A story told in a mirror" ("Myrrh: A Study of Persona ... " p. 96). We witness the truth, but cannot act upon it. But, "any time might be the time/we can look straight on/and break this lock/fettered to the thousands of years."

When you follow "the Greater Law," when you follow the orders of the poem, when you are strong enough to enter the Taboo, to break its "stricture," always the miracle happens: you encounter the Opposite, the Reversal — "Myrrh goes both ways." Turn around and face the Beast, the Aborigines have always known, and He will be your helper, his evil will dissolve. Good and Evil are NOT equal forces. As the Kabala says, "Evil is a shell that wraps around the Flame of Good." Iago, simply by his presence to the Lovers, those Good Beings, reacts. A natural, organic reaction. But in Judeo-Christianity, this becomes "free will," the Fathers' blackmail, lowly Evil. And we are unable to act.

We know Myrrha most, I think, in the beautiful "Petroglyph Poem." How satisfying (*satis:* enough) the weaving of the surfacely unrelated motifs and images of this poem. ("Lying down between pattern/and random scatter,/and I'll claim both," as Roche says in an earlier poem.) The ancient glyph on the rock: of the man in the doorway, post and lintel, the sun illuminating him, and the woman with a halo of sun, a child between them, running with antelopes. Sun is everywhere, this is the Dawn of Civilization, the *elan vital,* the substance of consciousness and nature. Then: the contemporary couple viewing the ancient glyph, she swimming in the night river, "his child, her child/bedded in separate houses" (of the privileged). "He wants to fuck her in an abandoned building," but this is "where some of the abandoned street children have children." The poet doesn't forget that children come from fucking, that there is no separation, now and then, between her lover, herself, her children, the Haves, the Have-nots, her Government. "She knows sometime/in the night there are winged creatures — angels" (the Myrrh). Sometime in the day she knows the angels are her "abandoned children/in a brick building ... children of children in no one's bed/constructive

9

grammar and stone." "Petroglyph Poem" — through the poem we must understand what is happening, we try to enter this incredible universe, the Story, a Line through this book — is about the unfathomable, unspeakable betrayal of the Myrrh, of the *elan vital,* of Life. The reason we suffer the Hunger that can't be sated is because out the window from our sheltered lovemaking are the starving. We are all connected. No matter how rich, Psyche knows, her father has her up for sale.

"How does the heart open?" THE LARGEST STEP IS THE ONE THROUGH THE MIRROR: to simply say it. "The Emptiness in which we know Desire does not seek to be filld but to fill" (Duncan, "Structure of Rime").

> . . . I started slow
> with vowels and each sound broke
> into song I'd waited to wail
> all my life, modulated into breathed
> stops and then again to open-throated
> full screams and swelling to shrieks
> throbbing at full cry and surging
> to deep sobs of every grief

You can't be a poet without being a Screamer, *thunder after thunder returning like history, like theater, like nightmare.* Like rhyme.

References

Robert Duncan, "Structure of Rime," *Ergo!,* Volume 3, 1988, Bumbershoot, Seattle.

Judith Roche, "Myrrh: A Study of Persona in H.D.'s *Trilogy,*" *Line* 12 : Fall 1988, Simon Fraser University, Vancouver.

Sharon Doubiago, Seattle, Washington
December 1992

HOT BONES

Welding
water and water
            on hot
welding
water and fire
bones
            hot bones
and a big box
a wall
                        a window in the wall

— Robin Roche —

MYRRH

It is measured in tears
Myrrha, *mar*, means bitterness,
       Myrrha, murmur, *mar*, the sea
             where love is born murmuring
of what's to be.
       A girl in bad trouble
       turns into a tree
       breaks open to birth
       a baby who becomes beloved of love.
       His blood becomes the anemone
            wind flower stained red.
       Her blood becomes myrrh,
       the tears of trees.
The smell of sorrow in some stories
          base chord for a mix of scents,
        myrrh deepens the floral
          and buries the dead.
The smell of love in others, as in
      I have perfumed my bed with myrrh, and
      the lover to be *anointed with oil of myrrh.*
It is, in any case, precious,
     a gift of potent   transformative
          potential.
Myrrh looks two ways at once,
     can go in any direction.

TRYING THE WAYS WE KNOW

We sat in the boat a long time.
The sky rippled grey,
then, apricot, then, later,
so bright we had to turn
our heads, look down.
All the dead fish anyone
ever ate swam through my mind.
I sang, "Salmon, salmon, salmon,"
over and over
in the only voice I was given
but it didn't help
and would have embarrassed you
if anyone heard me.
The sun kept hurting my eyes
and I began to feel the helpless arrogance
of slipping a tiny hook
in any random point
of this deep water
and expecting a fish
to jump on it. We kept on
reeling and casting
our thin lines.

DESIRE

Want is a less formal term than wish
but desire implies ardor —
as the waitress should not ask
if you desire wine —
wish implies more respect
and less lust.
Crave suggests a body necessity
such as thirst or hunger,
while covet is eager and envious,
spirit snared in content.
Passion has its roots in suffering
as desire has its in constellations of stars
but both tangle with rapture
— which shares a tap-root to ravish —
in movement toward ecstasy
to search the moment when flesh becomes smoke
and the boundaries of broken
form, trance-dance shape-shifting
through simultaneous layers of time
scattering dappled light let loose,
as the Passional is an account
of the sufferings of saints to be read
on the days of their festivals,
to prolong our desire
for desire itself
impulse enough

WHY SHE WENT TO THE WOODS

You do not know how I've spread out
    under those hands like melting butter.
I clung to the tree of a leg
    like flumed moss,
        bled on the floor
and mixed with ashes of my going down
in gritty hearths.
Embers, I've been, blowing myself
to life of shine and wood-grain,
babies sucking my spread fingers
while I put passions to rest
on my grandmother's folded blanket
where I found the musk and old-wheat
    of dried roses and crumbled letters.
If I've taken it to high arctic tundra
it was only because I needed the cold
    to think in.
If I've searched out purple stains
    on lichened rocks
it was only because I couldn't find
the green-wild eyes of wolves to drown in.
I've had to rub myself oily
on the stripped trunk of a bear-tree.

WE BALANCE EACH OTHER'S
NIGHT AND DAYLIGHT NEEDS

Dark falls by five and stays
long into tomorrow.
I drown it in wine and sleep,
leaden, until the wine wears off.
Then, instant insomniac, I have
hours to try to stop the terrors
of waking alone, though you are here
beside me and would wake gently
to listen to my litany of fears,
would give your arms, your smell
and murmurs. Finally, falling through long
space, night travelers, our bodies
link in loose weave of arms and legs,
joined at the hip like Siamese twins,
we joke — what it would be like to live
this way, horror of losing our separateness
wrapped round outside our heads and shoulders
like a shared aura of light. We hold
our pillowed heads so close we trade
breath and say we want to be
conspirators in inspiration
and pass a single Kool cigarette,
glowing back and forth in dark.
Greedy, I try not to hot-box it, rude
while sharing, blue-brown breath

inside me. How deep I want.
I speak the raving voice that attends
my waking night, sense lost in dark translation,
my cache of crowded need in works
clogging our dreams.

THEY THINK ABOUT ESCAPE

The sun rises red
and I become weary of your arms,
tongue brown with excess.
We've been yoked to the cart
of Hours, pulling the rough road,
ruts of night wheels.
This dull dawn
seeps to din of day,
   falls
      distracted
to glint of starry night,
so ambiguously beautiful.
But I'm easily seduced,
   all resolve unraveled.
Some bond unbroken, but tearing,
tethered by blue-veined flesh,
seed within soil,
some shattered scatter
of partial vision
searching, betrayed
by song of night
falling through grace
on loosened limbs —
pure act of extremity met
or only reached for,
and the road
still running.

AERIAL ESCAPE

I took a plane to Minnesota and gave my wrong name
the ticket taker never knew but you would have
recognized any new one I could choose
transferred to another line so hard
to remove my traces through pages
humming my idiomatic tunes with multiple name
changes an alias on each new ticket never knowing
what to declare
at the border I've walked
through fluorescent airports losing incriminating baggage
on the way though the allegory I come from
keeps recognizing me each time I execute
my amazing mid-air transfer

ANATOMY AND DESTINY

You said quantitative
  I said qualitative
but we lasted forever
   in the long night mountain caves and candles.
You said red roses
  I said sweet allysum
    and opened slow
  in purple iris with golden stamen.
  I licked your powdery gold dust and your legs
    twisted in my attracting pollen.
We took to sea in a boat
  where we rocked for aeons
    without touching ground,
  so close at sea to the stars,
    we became terrifying angels,
  feathers grew from steel pinions
   before they flattened
     to thin ends.
No one ever plans for addiction
  (carnal knowledge is absolute).
Now my hunger becomes quantitative
  and you hold me hard to my first word.
We're serving out our term of eviction.

LETTER HOME WHEN HOME HAS SHIFTED ON HER HAUNCHES

did we fail
again   to look
                        into each other's eyes
without flinching
someone lost nerve
in the heat of the making
            confused by the complex
                        of the mating
and we are promised
            to turn this wheel again
                        and again in aeons
circling   your fur
            grown shaggy   my breasts
loosened by time
            and so many to suckle
we'll flash taut again
            each turn new we'll believe
                        any time might be the time
we can look staight on
            and break this lock
fettered to the thousands of years
            refracted in our multiple eyes
                        mandala of failing vision
falling back on a damaged foresight

                    of amber eyes that glow
in the dark
                          we are
destined to lose
each other at the lake
              drag the river for our own remains
an old story we live
out of peripheral
vision

BASEMENT

You moved your body into my bed
your tools into my basement
— the fix-it-up-chappy —
you worked on everything I owned
till we were all in fine-tune,
temporary in our state of equilibrium,
perfectly poised at optimum essence.
After you left the first to go was Camille
the car, then the plumbing,
            dripping and leaking hot tears.
Now you come back to retrieve your tools
one at a time — always the handyman,
you can't resist fixing me up
(god knows I need work)
a little on each trip.
My mouth circles on you
and silences my stubborn song
of let me go lover, learned
to counter my bloody desire,
but your one-for-the-road
approach to maintenance
leaves me rummaging through
my own cluttered basement,
trying to sort out what's yours,
what's mine.

CAMILLE

the car has short-circuited
all her messages in the smell of burn
and plunder. I've been going to bed

with Charles Olson and glasses of wine
but she is demanding a mechanic's touch
and has taken to the road without me.

She wants me to read Baudelaire to her
screeching at sixty down the freeway,
the wine is optional but she wants flowers

slim and very *mal*, rotting in the back seat, smelling
of decomposed sweetness and deadly exhaust.
Vehicle of devastation, freewheeling flirt

of destruction, she shrugs off her seatbelts
and strains brake lines, her ignition
out of my hands. Last night

a policeman brought her home
drunken and reeling. I'd gone to bed
with Emily Dickinson and shocked

the cop with my own fits and starts, stut-
tering my apologies in dashes and fragments.
When he left we made our own peace with Bob

Dylan in the background. She was wild
and sobbing but her remorse
may be too late. Lover of excess, runner
of the world's highways, she's begging

to go to Grand Canyon again, saying she longs
to see the desert fruitful,
arid rocks in flow.

SHE SEARCHES

Let me pour myself on you like wine.
Let me rub myself on you like oil.
Let you rut in my fold like a rowdy he-goat.
Let you rain yourself on me from fertilizing clouds.
Let me gather rain in the hollow of my rose-mouth,
        let a drop of milky dew stay on the lip.
Let me climb you like a childhood tree.
Let me perch on top, a bird hovering,
        Isis-like, her search, for now, near sated.
Let you churn in my rocky coast like a violent sea.
Let me fly over your land forms, a desert wind
        scented with myrrh and maythorn.
Let me raise your temple pillar upright.
Let me welcome your green-milk glacial melt,
        terrifying torrent of summer break-up.
Let me hold even your ice floes
        until they melt in my warm hills.
Let you coax my sky-crested swallow
        until I gentle in your sky-streaming glory.
Let you glide your boat in my underground river,
        lose yourself in my fragrant forest.
Let me grow on you like green steamy ferns.
Let me ride your tongue right out of my earth
        into a crimson high keen cry.

THE SOUND I LEARNED FROM MY MOTHER'S SONG

In pre-uterine sight   the sea
before amniotic ocean
emergence   I remember
water, or was it sky
before the cave   the holy thighs
of my mother.
There must have been candles
on rock crags and the glow
of light through sacred bone
for I still see the rounded cone
of barrow where I was born
       sky of green leaves
shot through with golden sun.
Another mother held me rocking
on dry land   another island
in this inland sound
connection with ocean greater
than footsteps over our sand.
Her voice veiled in every murmuring
syllable of a mother's song.
      Go for the wildest blue
      whether ocean or air
I've heard each hidden
message she didn't know
she meant and passed it on
at every star or island I've made
a temporary mooring.

ALTERNATE INSOMNIA AT THE LAKE IN WINTER

I'm dreaming I can't sleep
and someone leads me to a balcony
to watch the morning
drench the lake,
a ploy to avoid an alarm that never comes.
I'm dreaming I'm awake,
all of me so hungry for a dream
I'm trying too hard to get
what I don't know I have.
A foot is touching mine
and I feel it in my sleep,
dreaming I'm awake and touching back
with eyes open in a room so dark
my iris can't accommodate.
I'm dreaming up insomnia,
black lake I drown in
and dredge the waters
to find my own body.

NIGHT PASSAGE

You talked in my dream and made me wait
until desire diffused from a central column and slid
into amoebas in all my limbs.
When I awoke the sheets were blood-soaked
but only in a small field, a red
anemone and I couldn't tell who had ended
us for now, you or me or the cat
who awakens me at three with his need
for the night, goring my sleep
for hours on end.
I flamed about above my body
hovering as we do,
on the lip of the oscillation,
falling headlong into a language
we make up but there
before we are, clothing
ourselves in stories of "love"
or "grief," the various fictions
of unknown names swelling
urgent under the tongue.
By the time the sky began to pale silver
then apricot, you had changed from man
to woman and we were both beasts of waiting
before we became birds of the morning
light, but heavy, with oiled feathers,

we struggled to fly before we thrust
ourselves alone but back into each other,
an ocean where we know how to swim.

DESIRE IN LAUGHING SEASCAPE

salt man never been here enough
I mean honey been bad hurt
had run barefoot along laughing seascape
trailed salt in sentence sing waves
sing water   sing salmon   sing she
said sing goddammit go get a god and help me
help me sing words when words when weather wild
wind blow hot below cold seascape sing sad so long
so grey so blowy blowzy hair all over stains on shirt
on skirt tacky shoes wants etched in face like lines
on glass it shows too much for tact
hearts on more than sleeves they shove in eyes
that register some specific portion of self abuse

gravity gone slack but the shape there showing through
some of the folds so cool but it still shows
how bad she wants hard she tries mouth
a cave of open bruised opening and eyes
eyes unwise history written
but the times she went down hands casting and fingernails
grasping believing this might be the time in the color
of the depth of the eyes so deep someone could drown
in the debris not able to swim for all those broken off
dead branches where shoots extend hope hardened in bare air
before it breaks to float deadened in the waters of those eyes

ten scars make a woman and you have to eat a peck of dirt
before you die she remembered hardened green branching
blanching to pale brown cut off from the source and not
grown far enough to reach are new ones on her
if there weren't so many collecting so long
it wasn't for lack of trying it shows on flesh
each stretch mark mute mouth to its maker
history is written on the body
each tear torn
from its socket of bone and soft tissue
salt water erodes what it touches
yet it is the fluid of life
the sea within

HELEN: WHEN THEY CALLED HER WITCH

In all the stories I'm either on the wall
or on my back — that siren call
echoing in my ears and I can hardly walk
through town for all the eyes.

I'll perfect my disguise,
            rare version of bitch mask
            rendered in worked leather,
and paint their roofs with pale gold

Splashed moon beams. I'll ride
those wet roofs into their back yards
and serve them drugged dinners
until they find intrigue in their own minds

And leave mine alone.

I have slipped some law but lie under another.
Something born beneath the bone,
a structural grammar of dream,
anonymous spirals of stored memory.

It's story seen in a mirror
I follow when I rattle at the barriers
and push at boundary stones
beyond where cracks have closed.

I am famous for walking walls,
lying down between pattern
and random scatter,
and I'll claim both.

They are deciding I'm a minor goddess,
esoteric knowledge, a sort of Etta James
instead of Bessie Smith. Good
but not big time. My stars

Rise and fall like August nights,
on my back in hot sand, taking in
meteor showers, and scholars
worry about my mother, my swan-engendered

Beginnings, rapture and beating of wings from before
my birth imprinted on the line of my limbs.
It's me in love with the sweet sax love line
they forget, silence between the notes,

Phanos, tied to but slipping
fertile earth when I go beyond,
            flesh loosened, then left,
and how each one, pushed far enough,

Goes back to the same sea, Mar, Mère,
the blue of all the open sky.

DENDRITES

I am Helen of the Trees,
>which means they hang me from them.
>>(no, no. It is puppets they hang.)

I am Helen of the Trees,
>which means they beat me with a wooden stick,
>>or a branch switch.
>>(no, no. It means you write with a wooden
>>>pencil, weave with a wooden loom.)

I am Helen of the Trees,
>which means if they cut me in half
>>you could count my rings to see
>>>how old I am.
>>>(no. horrible. But you are from before time.)

I am Helen of the Trees,
>which means I sail away in a wooden boat.
>>(but all boats were wood then, and you
>>>sailed away with lovers.)

Alone, I pitch and toss my head like an ocean. My hair flows green. Birds talk to me forever. I hatch babies I don't raise. My roots grab fists of deep earth, hold on tight and suckle. Bees bring me heavy golden pollen. I spread my arms above lovers lying under me. The sky rides over me and I become fertile with inseminating rain. My babies fly on wings of wind. I grow large and lithe. I grow ripe and bear fruit, which falls from me. I am the reflected green of the sound I follow down and up at the same time, roots and branches into cleft beauty. My blood crystallizes into stones. I am form for flames.

LOVE IN A LIFEBOAT

He holds my bones too hard
as if they were birds about to fly.
I understand his shuddering sighs,
shaking loose a grief so long and harsh
he breaks open at my touch.
He breaks open for me to see
a tangled viscera I could heal
at what expense . . .
What witch is called forth
to walk a ceremonial corridor,
desperate labyrinth I want to leave
and what do we have to do for each other
in recurrent dream of unclean history,
flocks of birds forming,
      wheeling and flying off
in pattern I can't follow
        from the swell of the waves
           where I'm awash
              immersed in rise and fall.

HELEN: THE QUESTIONS

And what of she who died for favorable winds?
What lesson did my girl learn from death
                              come so close?
My sister's child and she
                              within weeks of each other
had shown first blood.
We made a fire circle,
we four, circling our own drama
on the threshing floor, the girls
holding hands, laughing,
                    embarrassed, shy and flushed
at the intimacy of the occasion.
We sang our song
to welcome first flow
and destiny, not knowing
what we forecast —
a knife to open her neck,
to bleed her dry on an altar —
                    mockery of our ceremony.
And what of our grief
with me not there to hold
my sister and my girl through the terrible night.
Always we have taught the teaching.
What of my girl? What will
she learn from a mother

who isn't there — that the way
to be a woman is to follow
love in a lifeboat, rocking
on the roll of a blue, blue sea?
Will she hear of my famous
beauty, how even a simple
sandal looks strapped
thinly around my ankle
but not how the open-awed vowel sound
flows through the echo chamber
of the heart?
Will they tell her I use drugs
but forget to say how I know poppies,
that my potions are to heal a fevered
mind, crack open an armored heart?
Can she learn to read the birds in flight
without me? They will teach the lesser law —
a dangerous stricture of structure —
without the inner form
of the Greater Law.
No one has told the truth
about me. No one
has had the words.

BUT IT TAKES TILL THEN

All theater is seduction,
the cowboy's swinging dance in the bars,
the mud and sawdust grimed floors,
the boots used to walking anywhere,
high work on steel beams,
dried roses stuck behind every picture in the house,
traces of streets with flower-sellers, samba clubs,
                              and African hashish.
The rain swells the stream and moans into river,
the moon reaching its fullness now.
In a night or two,
        I'll walk and walk and walk
        and sometimes I'll run
                just because it feels so good,
like salmon, the strongest meat,
red with multiple roe and ripeness.
Angel beating heavy wings at all my openings.
They opening slow. By morning
I've given it all.

DANCING DREAMS MY MOTHER HAD, I IN UTERO

My mother lay on the couch
in thick September heatwave,
bloated, distended with me
while her spiritbody rose
through air, sailed out the open door,
swooped and hovered
like some giant transparent hummingbird
over the empty lot across the street.
My mother skimmed the seeded tips
of tall weeds while I,
ecstatic in my amnion,
tumbled over and over,
sea-born somersaults
in weightless free fall,
kinesthetically gleeful
arabesques in amniotic ocean,
my whole body haired with tiny wings,
my mother, pure spirit, freed for now.
It was only days later I learned
the ripping force of push and breath,
                leaden stop of gravity.

MYRRHA

He is a tree trunk.
I am a snake curving around
his neck, under his arms,
around his belly, in his lap.

He smells leather, tobacco, bread,
coriander, *kore-andros*.
I rub against his bristly whiskers,
my face burrowing into his neck.

I can't get close enough.
He laughs his tickling whiskers
into my neck. I wiggle
and squirm around his tree trunk

all giggle, shriek, and want.
Small snake me. Mermaid me,
my tail all curvilinear line and squirm.
He's had enough and hands

me back to her — narcissus and lavender,
sun dried sheets, her soft skin
smooth where he bristled. Both, the smoke
of burned tear, earthy aftertaste of wild honey.

We rock on the boat of their bed
but when he stands up
I see the other of him
by accident. Something

like wrinkled fruit, something
like a hangman's noose, loose,
grotesque animal, its ferocious
power sews my eyes with stitches to its spot.

BETWEEN PATTERN AND RANDOM SCATTER

*will I find myself trained to believe
everything,
as our fathers, the scientists, have been
trained to deny?*

— Robert Duncan —

THREE

—1—

We were
standing just outside
of sanity,
hitchhiking both ways
at the same time.

—2—

Approaching sorrow I do not speak,
am free to come and go as I choose,
yet each day the old men in me
ride a little closer to stone.

—3—

Here a tangled park
overgrown
with aging mountains
fat on crescent moons
run rivers
rich in delta silt.

AFTER SLEEP

The last time I came down
    the mountain trail
I searched for your trace
    in violets and anemones,
knowing you prefer the littlest flowers
    barely out of leaf-mould in damp ground
and your scent would linger for me
under and over the sky smell
    of small blooms.

When I found the flowers trampled
I knew it wasn't you
who stepped, though your pads are broad.
Oh love, my season is coming full
    on me again. Which trail
did you follow in the last migration
and where
will you find spring?

CIRCLES

To say that we three have become
a we even though she doesn't know
about me. Since he is a kind
of a husband, she has become
a kind of a wife and, in a way,
we are all living the same life.
And the two collections of children,
two he's, two she's, a set for each,
are also in relation and that
the he's know each other in play,
which forms another family.
Though the she's have never met,
I've met his she and he mine,
we both know each other's he
and we constantly compare our relations
to our children.
It can get even more complex
when I think of all my other he's
who have become husbands
because once they cross that corner
and become Eternal Persons of the marriage bed
in Imagination there's no turning back.
But then there are all their other wives
and children, former and subsequent, with their own stories,
plus all our mothers, fathers, sisters, brothers,

grandmas and grandpas, making our erotic acts of meeting
generate not only poems
but a sort of sweet connection
of families without end.

REQUIEM
For Woody

This body of fate we carry around
      with us is what we call God,
some improvisation we act on outline,
          the best we can.
Your death to us another country,
farther away than the stars,
     your life among us a haunted song,
         call and response between us,
rhythm of the intricate dance we've done
on the clearing ground   arena
    in the heart of a forest
        we can't see.

And are done, for now, and put to rest
in wake of final boat and friends carrying bone and ash,
in wake of wind we bring your story
    and scatter your song.
In water you lie awake
like the whale we once saw
    from your boat alone and sounding.
In water, lie awake alone
    on wind
blown below the island sky and wailing.
Sea-spin and sink and mingle,
    water

awash with bone and ash, wake behind
the boat to carry his body,
wind to wind
down from ground of living
        a life we loved.

THE RELEASE

The truth is only an example
of what lies blurred beyond
the shattered heart.
The boy said he loved her
as he shot his seven bullets.
She left quickly but not entirely.
            Suddenly open
she slipped like liquid
out a broken mirror
running with the blood
of a burst heart,
reflected in the many images
left on the ground
    each one saying
        "I want my . . . "
mother, it would have been
But she wasn't there.
She streamed through
a difficult transition,
caught in bone
    an hour and a half
        at the threshold,
suddenly crowned clean
    and was gone so far
so fast our eyes failed us.

We huddled together and tried
to wave but gravity made
each gesture clumsy,
suffering, as we were, the colors
of refracted light.
Heavy, as we are,
in our sad clothes.

GREEN RIVER

(for Elisa Tissot, 1962-1984)

I don't know just where the bones were buried
but I know what he looks like.
   . . . today in the Green River Gorge because the walls
      were closing in at home,
               that true for me now, early autumn
and twelve days into the teacher strike,
      my son and I searching escape
on any riverbank we can run to.
      True for forty-three women,
               girls I can't help feeling here
                       walls-closed-in at home
               who ran
street-side and came to some end
of truth at this riverbank
here and there downstream
and up, in little piles
each case with its similarities
studied and recorded by a large task force
of police searching for truth
      and I imagine everything so true now
      for the women there can be no truth
      because there is no opposite.
(Slant of sun on water making
a more burning shine than summer)
Somewhere by this river shore with its own
      rock walls rising over me
(water-carved cup holes all around), filled fresh

with the river's own rising
and I almost think I see spirit-girls
drinking from rock-rounded bowls.
I know what he looks like
because he won't stay out of my dreams
and I have some experience with killers
having watched one for three weeks
in a courtroom and though I don't see his face
anymore I will never forget a certain slant
of shoulder when viewed from behind
and imagine you can tell a killer
by slant of shoulder though there must be other
similarities besides what they leave behind
    for parents to pick up.
But then, even shoulders must look different
when they raise the gun
or do whatever this one does
who won't stay out of my dreams,
the flat blond look of cheek and eye-ridge
    now burned in memory
In dreams he's an actor
and I'm not afraid for myself
but for all the young girls
who aren't buried with roses
and a pink party dress
but borne out in burlap bags
though she, as well as they,
are, by now,
    bodies of bone.

AFTER THE REVOLUTION

We know now, having the babies
would be bad for the country.
We have been waiting
for grass to grow
but so many feet trod
the new shoots
to grey mud
and we see no green.
Now they have planted
government trees
on the long steppes
to slow the wind
in its ancient testing
of our city
and we know it's long
labor with hard pains
to birth
this nation
each of us growing
as so much grass. They plant
the green belts to give us air,
our many coal fires eat up
our own oxygen while warming
our winded bodies running
to catch up to ourselves.

Old Ways burn low and strong
as cooking braziers though
we are building a new world.
My mother-in-law was young
when liberation came but remembers
how she fought, her friends
so brave and dying for the struggle,
and so thinks women now,
soft. She fought for freedom.
We have only the task
of keeping breath in it.

THE OPEN BOOK COMES OFF THE PAGE

It's a long and narrow hallway.
I've been told not to open doors.

I am the young wife of the story
and have an innocent charm.

My fatal flaw is my curiosity.
It's been set up that way.

Tied to my finger is a sisal string
also tied to a brass doorknob.

Its third end is tied to a loose tooth
which makes a hollow rattle in my head.

Any movement of the door will make me
a snaggle-toothed old witch.

My husband's bristly beard
is knotted in long loose strands

beneath my dress to my cunt,
which is warming to all the attention.

Arachne couldn't create such tangled web
for a flyfisher-king who's sprung his reel.

My slightest twist turns pain for the sentient doorknob,
the rooted tooth, and trickles blood on the chin.

It's then that I remember knives, my kitchen companions,
scissors, my sewing room sisters,

shivs, my streetwalking costume,
and surgery, which I've practiced in my dreams.

The chin scars and falls on its face,
the door breaks, and the tooth rots in place.

THUNDER AFTER THUNDER, RETURNING LIKE RHYME

It could have been called history.
It had all the marks: blood on the walls,
steel shards blooming in flesh in riotous colors,
people marched blindfolded along a road
the feet didn't recognize, nowhere journey
usually ending at a bloated river,
the earth scorched and the wells poisoned.

It could have been called theater,
with its classic theme of struggle against fate,
it medieval undertones of Passion Plays, Feasts of Fools,
fiery ritual of *auto-da-fe,*
echoed addition of the Inquisition,
its cadenced words soaring on wings of extremity
the gods would have appreciated
if they happened to be listening.

It could have been called nightmare
with its birth in stars and rusting memory,
shreds clinging to bone and promise of water
broken in the sour taste of the denouement,
coming, as it does, before and after and before
the silence and slow time circle
concealed in the half-smile.
"Death itself instructs."

SOCIAL SECURITY

(This is not all true)
The words break into their own bayonets and bread.
I remember hope that season of snow and ice and fire —
hoses Henry Ford turned on the crowd at the gates
in January and water froze to their drenched clothes.
I make Hudsons and write fire.
I am to learn the intricate rules of social
security to teach others.
                              (what I remember of what she
                              remembered to tell me)
We are gathering for siege, the men on one side,
women on the other. No breath of scandal
can be in our struggle.
                              (memory is the mother)
We sang Solidarity Forever for three days
and stayed inside the walls we seized,
I slipped in and out, passing
messages and bringing food.
                              (I know that but I don't know
                              what they won)
Mexico is an imaginary state of my mind but in 1933
Diego is painting the winter walls of Detroit
                              (mural of memory of my childhood —
                              she made me look)

Frida blooms in tropical costume on the society pages,
    thrilling flower of flounced red skirt,
she shocks our good taste ethic.

                        (she knows of Diego but not of Frida)
but has a miscarriage in dark stains on hotel sheets.
I wear only beige.
I've had no baby but my body is gathering self for conception.

When he comes he will already have traveled to Russia,
                        (he brought back boxes of pictures—
                        tractors, great churches, girls in
                        babushkas. I remember he only
                        knew how to ask girls to go to
                        bed with him in Russian — but
                        how would I know that?)
his bourgeois view of Kansas French-Catholic farm life broken
in shattered shards with spaces between
    to allow some flow of plasma
            where we will meet and swim
upstream river
of tense
I've waited for all my life.
                        (she wore other colors)
He will promise to take me to Mexico.
                        (in the eleventh year he did —
                        four hours in Juarez, with a
                        taxi waiting)

The color of my dress will be ashes-of-rose.
Three little girls will gallop in a herd around my house.
I will teach them dreams of flowers and songs of a Union Maid.
One of them will tremble at the kitchen table,
eyes streaming tears, she will sob with no subject
                              (sob with no subject)
    though our telling will be of Arthur and Guinevere.
It will confuse him. I will feel her wild joy.

                              (they got the TV to watch the
                              McCarthy hearings. They held
                              hands and feared their own history.
                              She married him for his seed and
                              his travel and his careless dark
                              eyes.)

TRYING THE WAYS WE KNOW

And he heard, as it were, the echo
of an echo in a shell,

words neither sung nor chanted
but stressed rhythmically;

the echoed syllables of this spell

— H.D. —

TRYING THE WAYS WE KNOW, PART II

First we build a fire,
then we prepare our objects.
One of us has stones
    one of us has words
        written on hand-made paper
    one of us has feathers.
One says no. It's bad
    to burn a feather.
Because this is new (old) to us
we are thankful
some(one) knew and saved
that bad from being.
We bury feathers
    though the ground is frozen,
burn the stone and words
    (set free)
and then we start to sing.
It's broken song
    (some start stumbling)
and cracked voices crescendo
at the end
like a quest(ion) escaped.

APRIL

Oh familiar dark ground
I come back to you
core and Kore
on my back
in meadow again
both seed and earth
I am rent
with the ruthless
opening

THE FLOWERS

When you ask them
what they do for a living
they do not mention photosynthesis
but unfurl their slender petals
spread them
like a slow dance move
throb a sweet surge
of deep scent
unsound the shadow
of a sob

THE NIGHT WE HOLLERED DOWN
THE TUNNEL IN THE DELL

You said there's a poem in there,
like a hollow well with water
deep down the sound
bouncing on a rounded wall,
moonlight stunning our lungs
to life and some lusty yelling
circle dances we spiraled,
stomping and clapping,
wild October fragrance fermenting plums
singing an earthy wine on the ground.
She, ten years old and half as tall as me,
twirling on a stump in a clearing,
all of us moonburnt, shown up
in bright night light,
you, in silence silhouetting our loud sound,
somewhat accustomed, by now, to mine,
but amazed at your daughter's
little wild heart.

THE FOREST AT NIGHT AND ON INTO

mornings they crowd in
at the watering hole
leaving little room
for my most simple needs
they jostle my dreams
while walking through slatted shadows
they erase my antecedent and place
my position somewhere else
a point beyond in air
referent to what I don't know
and can't find out
slanting along desire
as the day runs out
each clue catch is incomplete
color with no name
flowing formless
in dust of earth-light
fragments that suddenly blaze
with flash of silver hiss of silk
they fall in colder twilight
leaving my tongue hungry
a series of slow shards
crumbled silent in my hand
a damaged set of instructions
quiet as the dead

THE BONES OF THE PRIESTESS LOOM LARGE
ON THE BEACH

(for H.D.)

In the hollow of rib cage —
the most astounding blue sky
laced by ladder of white bone
light wind blue blows through.

Wind sounds these bones
in madrigal tunes.
The ear hears in its chambered whorl,
voice swirl with echoed voice.

Sound billows bellow in broken space
vibrate the empty room that held the heart.
The bones of the priestess, a harp
in this sharp wind of bleeding layers

of all the air has held
of whispers and cries, sound
and letter, shaping my view of the sky
in blue through bleached cage bone.

THE BAIT
(for R.L.C.)

in a dream   in a dream
you came as the angel Gabriel
but I couldn't remember
your name   you didn't look
like you but I knew
by several clues   first
what I called you came suddenly
though you corrected me
and gave me a gift
picture of yourself
which didn't look like
you   very young
your hair rising like a dark forest
from a pale forehead
(that was a telltale sign)
like a French film star
but different in real
life if that was
real if this is
you said several times
Gabriel to teach
me the name angel
of annunciation we were
in a big ferry boat
with earth loam underfoot

preparing to cast off
on Northern waters
in a line-rigged little fishing skiff
we caught fat green snakes
we dug in the earthy deck
to use as bait
they looked dangerous
writhing and flashing
like that
even their dust prints
came alive

LOVERS

(after Jack Spicer)

"To begin with, I could have
slept with all the people in the poems" —

which doesn't mean I could
people the poems

but more I sleep in the poem
as a wolf in the water

— who arise and go now, leaving me
lattice of form as they pass through

the lace. And become alone
with an insufficient vocabulary,

holes and shaped space,
insurmountable distances

and lovers who sometimes leave
whole sentences on my lips

before they disappear
to the deeply dangerous snow

without door, hand, mirror
or recognizable syntax

and the wine too green
to drink the altarstone unbloody.

I could have slept
with all the people in the poems

and did, in a way,
but it was premature,

still distilling the wine
long open-eyed nights

of repeated, unknown phrases,
recurring bickering phonemes

blanking out to white silence
before I can find the pattern,

the people in the poems
as bloody as my own body.

THE WHITE HORSE GIRL AND THE BLUE WIND BOY

The boy lives at the back of the wind
    and swirls in his dust cloud.
The girl lives on the cave of rocks
    by the sea.
When the tide comes up
she washes out to sea and sprays white,
    like flower-forms on lips of waves.
She lives in purple water.
He lives in amber air.
He comes riding thunder and darkened light.
She is riding herself in the wild, wild waves
    of heavy horses in the sea.
He comes making the wind
go over your head
and your hair fly in the air.
She turns colors: first turquoise,
    then obsidian maelstrom.
When you swallow her you can't breathe.
He cuts quartz in the rocks
    and opens up cracks in granite.
When you swallow him you can't breathe.
She is hot in the sea.
The Wind Boy takes his wind
to her water
to cool her

and to make her go
    flying fast in the waves.
The Horse Girl flings herself forward —
    hoof to hand they fly
    falling like scattered stars,
hanging like hope in a dream.
When you swallow it you can't breathe.

PETROGLYPH POEM

—1—

Blue clouds bleed mist
    mountains in the distance
meaning rain to the east
a man stands in a doorway
    post and lintel
the sun illuminates him
a woman with a halo of sun
    antelopes run
carrying curved horns
    the flow both
ahead and behind
staghorn figure in the middle of a spiked sun
    stars bloom around
a child stands on two legs
    running between figures
facing front on flat land
circle signs in spokes
            she is sun
a spider spins the story out
despite shadow and cloud changing the light
    high wind rising ryegrass
        whipped waters offshore
sun is everywhere

the woman has a halo of moon
    she swims the night river
he stands on the shore in jeans
    he sits on the dock
her empty clothes spill in a pile before him
    his clothes still shaped to his body
his child   her child
    bedded in separate houses
horses on the wind ride the river path
    silver light
which defines the dark
    they will walk in a forest
    barely lit by far-off street lights
    until her wet hair dries
when he called he said
    where were you
        I've been bleeding
she won't bleed for two weeks
they will go to a house
    where she will be launched on a journey
          and he will meet her there

he wants to fuck her in an abandoned building
she sees its old brick and blinded windows
she wonders what clothes to wear

it is not an idle question
they are driving by
    that building
            old brick   blinded windows
                    children sleeping
some of the street children
have children   the city
has taken the park benches away

they are driving by
heading east in evening inventing
sunset streams in bands behind
their children sleeping
in separate houses

it's summer and they can sleep outside
they will go to the lake

before the sleeping
on the deck of a house
they will drown in dreams of horses

before they dream they will merge
each in a separate mind
they will try to share it

she will wake in the night
and want to walk barefoot to his bedside
but he will be right there

trying to bridge the chasm
when he's so close
she will sleep again

he wants to fuck her in an abandoned building
she wonders what abandonment means
and tries every kind

but she knows   sometime
in the night there are winged creatures
she won't think of the word *angel*

until after breakfast
it will be a word
unlike what happened in the night

sometime in the day
she will think of abandoned children
in a brick building

blind windows   the benches
and children of children in no one's bed
constructive grammar and stone

CHANGING ON THE ROAD

Early morning psyche's feet stay in sleep
and you won't stay out of my dreams,

your high wire act cut to a car
where I change my clothes in front of a stranger,

back seat embarrassment,
while you say you know how to find a cave

where quartz crystals are lodged upstream.
The stranger watches impassively

but I know what he's thinking,
eye of my own superego on me and my uneasy anarchy.

You wade in the water and pick out perfect crystals,
translucent pointed mysteries of frozen light.

What's more you can cook our lunch with an unattached
light bulb, too obvious connection to power.

My sister has joined us in long legs and short shorts
that barely cover her blond pudendum

but she is happily married and not bothered
by what exposes me, my hands halfway

between underpants and nylons under my skirt,
driving down a dirt road tunneled toward dark.

LETTER TO LI T'AI-PO

Where are you now, my love?
I lie alone in the dark, growing old.
— Li T'ai-po —

all of us alone
some of us
not all the time
alone
whatever
the square root radical
some of us are in this
together
alone
and some
times even
alone together
a sum
dear friend

PINNIPEDIA

As in a dream I remember my old grown-over gill slits
   salmon breath
         seal swim, smooth-sided flips,
firm as any sea mammal flesh.
Hungered lean fast hunt,
   fresh fish snapped mid-stroke,
my long watery whiskers streaming
   sea-sped on flash runs
arcing from shoal to shoal of island rock,
air filled with feathered wing,
heard hunting bird by flocks of thousands,
sun-blue noisy with cutting cry
bursting, shine scattered
   (sheer joy of light)
lung-hungered air inspired
   above
        steep fall
   swelling wave.

MY LIFE IN LETTERS

My life consists of cutting out precise parts of myself
and mailing them off to the universe. They return, mostly
battered and rejected. A very few find parties to attend,
where they lift their heels, drink wine, and dance the can-
can. Those blessed ones swarm in several dawns later with
flushed faces, wilted roses, and crushed skirts. They don't
tell their stories but lift cold, salt-sprayed kisses to my
lips. Nights I wander the city looking for stragglers. They
alight at bars where crystal glints and chimes, talk to strangers
in brick-lined alleys, deep-fish from the public dock. I glimpse
from shadows but do not interfere. Who knows where they go once
they leave the post office? Surely they don't have enough sense
to come in out of the rain! Not that I mind the cold but it is
difficult to feel pain in a part several states away. Not that
I think their journeys will be without pain.

WE TAKE A NIGHT BOAT RIDE TOGETHER

It's a dark night and we have to walk
beyond the curve to see the moon,
mist-risen and blue-rimmed
but round as a long life.
We walk slowly along the brink
like two tentative shore birds
about to sail forth.
I support much of your slight weight
on black sand. Gritty textured,
it slips away under our feet.
Moon finds pale glint of phosphorescent shine
at the borders between what we know
and sea in void of nothingness.
It's the borders that confuse us,
their thin flare of ghost plankton
neither material nor dream,
and that we don't know
where we go but out
there in the Sound,
pushing our small boat
toward hidden islands,
black shapes,
layer behind layer.

PARTHENOS

— after Sappho —

Virgo state verging
on any ocean island
unoccupied emergence

We lived on an island,
made our house
of quince, of pomegranate,
wove hyacinths in our hair.
We relearned the art
of anointing with oil —
clean woolen robes,
unbleached and at ready.
In amber   in crimson light
at night we sang circles
around each star-eyed visitor,
our song wings
circling the earth,
boundaries of port
in any storm,
we were grace
to every guest.
Each morning they left
in ships, cleansed
with our scent,

lavender and sea,
ribbons in their sails.
Our island intact,
we went on with our work.

MNEMOSYNE

In the passage of time
memories develop their own memory
born of star placement and rust
until we can't tell
if we remember the event
or its re-telling.
Even we carbon-based creatures
flake away in fragments
like an old house falling apart
in a slow motion film,
a cathedral changing
from one deity to another
and then another, each
with a name, a genesis
and a history of hard birth
in the parent-god,
now erased or repudiated,
and gathering theorems
like the antiquated geometries
of exquisite angels
breathing their own breath
into a dance we did once.

MY LIFE AS A SCREAMER

can you deny
mouthfuls of blackened blood
I spit out
             each morning
to sing?

— Diane di Prima —

MY LIFE AS A SCREAMER

Some people don't believe in trolls.
They hide in plain sight
so are easy to miss
in the open along the borders
between the dark tangle of Douglas Fir
and the long stretch of sea opening ocean.

She was bleeding and she started by fingerpainting
his body with blood before
they walked in the sea.
She ran the beach ankle deep
in salt water and felt the lift of wings
as shore birds rose, a gull
girlfriend flew over and cawed,
    I'll tell you about him later.
She wanted all the gossip she could get
    but was finding out her own ways.
Of the sea she said . . . major hypothermia plans
for me but I'll slide out
from under with my agility.

He was talking to the trolls by then
and he never told what they said
but she was touching flower openings
pale green and pink sea anemones

to watch them shudder and contract
because she knew they liked it.

When they found the cave
he didn't want to go in,
the rock too big, trolls contained
potent oppressive potential.
She took his hand to the inside in the hollow
of the sound cave,
sound around, rock walls resonant
rosette faces in the wall.
　　　Look, they've left their jewelry on the floor
　　　　　　the kind they wear.
They favor gold and precious stones,
interlacing chains and glitter,
they make it out of mud and bones.
It is the thing of no practical use
that stirs their hearts. Humans
have tried to steal their gold,
only to find, on getting it home,
that it has become its original form.

He tried to get her to leave the cave,
uncomfortable for him,
she started singing a low note,
an *aieee,* an *ahhh* which grew
and deepened, then rose, a sound
aloud allowed loud in every
niche and fold of rock wall

magnified, writ large in sound
allowed loud and shattering.
He left, walked out the oval opening
to sunlight and sea and she was
alone with loud sound.

Fear came into her scream and she felt need
for birth from rock walls to light and water.
She knew she could scream until she shattered
and broke into small shards and never be whole again:
broken form stretched into repressed strain for silence
from scream and she stopped it, stuffed it,
and bore herself out of the sound cave.
Her life as a screamer stopped
from childhood out-of-control
when her mother
would take her shoulders gently,
look directly in her eyes and say
 you don't need to do this you don't
 like it when you can't breathe.
And she learned to control the screaming.
        Even as a child
she knew another mother might have slapped
her screaming face and she never could have stopped it.
Recurrent story. A man slapped her screaming early on
and she didn't do it again with him.
Her daughter stopped her in a church,
the *aieee* from the deep well,
the funeral of a dead girl.

When her mother died, she dismantled her house
of scarves, jewels, and books, and that time
her sister stopped the rising swell
and she was grateful.

Out in the open again, he
talked to the most massive trolls,
born of stone,
but they walked back along the shore
and she picked up a long bull-whip kelp
to feel its firm smooth flesh, swung it around
her head until it sang its loud whistle-whirr
song of sound and air cut and shaped
and finally wrapped itself around her legs,
stung her sharply and made a deep red welt,
a mark that stayed.
    I didn't do that, he said,
                    but I'll get the blame for it.
Naked now, they walked into the sea
waves breaking on bared breasts
    and deeper they went,
                the sea fog blurring the shore
    big waves crashing
                she could scream again each time
                        they broke over her
    the cold a force luring them on
                        and on deeper
    cold reaching the bones
                but strangely wonderful

                    cold   cold   I love you   cold
            the waves recurrent rhythm
        force they flowed under
                        forgetting . . .

They looked behind to see beach blurred in fog,
an eerie calm in the water stretched back to shore
and sudden knowledge that they'd been seduced too deep
for ordinary safety   one more deeper, they said silently,
and she cound scream again, open throated joyous surprise
each time it broke over her overwhelming anything she thought
she knew with new knowledge of sea   and more and more,
one
more again until there was no time left and they turned
together back to shore and found the earth
with their feet.   Terra firma sang the feet
deep in warm sand.
shi shi beach
shi shi, the sand sang back, shi shi
shi shi
edge walking on the western rim.

            there was a kiss like elfin bread
            he said   she said   they kissed
            like elfin bread

    At first I didn't know where
    to be
    in the cave

(the second time)
she went in again
alone
and left a message

hollowed in sound
sound around
resonating on the rosette faces
in walls, gargoyles, womb cave
of my mother, I started slow
with vowels and each sound broke
into song I'd waited to wail
all my life, modulated into breathed
stops and then again to open-throated
full screams and swelling to shrieks
throbbing at full cry and surging
to deep sobs of every grief
I've ever known in my story
then again beyond my own
the tale of the tribe
told whole
and finally
a deep pitched growl
that climbed the scale transformed
into full animal roar blasting
my being to a dreadful thunderburst
of everything any of us ever endured
or leap into with startled
open eyes.

As it subsided
it resolved slowly
into a cadenced
diminuendo of wild sounds
finding time and tune
and eventually,
after everything else,
word.

The words can't be recorded here.
Prayers and promises
and then silence
unpronounceable   unutterable
ineffable
silence
that hummed electric
indwelling
along rock walls
re-sounding
in the hollow chamber.

How does the heart open?
The deepest ground the ground of sound.

When she was finished
she was quite finished.
She saw the oval opening empty with light
beyond the folded furrows of passage
and walked to its rim,

opening to seascape horizon,
trolls receding, grey-blue shadows
in the open, along the borders.

Later he made her scream again
but it was like the sea did it,
breaking over her in waves,
cresting in pure exuberance.

HOSTIA

It became clear that they were to eat her.
She understood the process and could have refused
but entered willingly. No one could say what it meant.

It would take a long time. She was to eat food
for the dead, then become dead food.
Each night she descended a long staircase

to pomegranates and apples, fish and wine,
little cakes gathered from crossroads.
Children cheerfully helped their mothers make them.

She now slept all day in dreams of willow and barley.
Photographers kept taking pictures of her.
It was taking longer than she had imagined.

Months along someone asked, was she always this size?
Underneath, we answered, but not on the surface.
The dreams changed to wicker bundles.

A child asked, have we done this before?
Hush, murmured the mother, we've always done this.
Transformation of waste is our oldest preoccupation.

She descended nightly, flesh naked and shimmering,
staircase of angles and successive planes,
her meals more urgent lumps on night's table.

Episodes of deja vu from dreamtime days,
grown vast on moonfood and seed;
she prepared for their feast of flesh.

Spring was coming swiftly
mixing memory and smoke
we knew to be lies leading

to deeper rhythm surging
underneath our sour masks,
our dry rocks beaten to dull drums.

Hyacinths were pushing out of cold ground.
Risers and treads of nighttime manna
creaked with weight of voluptuary sweetness.

Dangerous bread of your bread,
sacra. *You don't know what bitter salt —*
what fertile seed I'll be, taken inside.